INTRODUCTION

MILESTONES OF FLIGHT

SPACE HALL

AIR TRANSPORTATION

BORN TO FLY

MILITARY USE OF AIRCRAFT

QUEST FOR NEW FRONTIERS

This edition published in 1995
by SMITHMARK Publishers Inc.
16 East 32nd Street
New York, New York 10016.

SMITHMARK books are available for bulk purchase
for sales promotion and premium use. For details
write or telephone the Manager of Special Sales,
SMITHMARK Publishers Inc., 16 East 32nd Street,
New York, NY 10016. (212) 532-6600

Produced by Brompton Books Corp.,
15 Sherwood Place,
Greenwich, CT 06830

ISBN 0-8317-6758-8

Printed in China

10 9 8 7 6 5 4 3 2 1

THE NATIONAL AIR AND SPACE MUSEUM

TEXT	BARBARA ANGLE HABER
DESIGN	ALAN GOOCH, DESIGN 23

SMITHMARK

In memory of my mother, Ruth Donley Angle

Acknowledgments
The author and publisher would like to thank the following people who helped with the preparation of this book: Alan Gooch of Design 23, the designer; Rita Longabucco, the photo editor; and Jean Martin, the editor.

1 *At the dedication of the National Air and Space Museum on July 1, 1976, in the bicentennial year of the country's founding, President Gerald Ford declared it, "A perfect birthday present from the American people to themselves."*

INTRODUCTION

Each year, on the last weekend of windy March, kites pepper the sky near the Washington Monument. Sponsored by the Smithsonian Institution, the Kite Flying Festival grants prizes to the most creative and best-flying entries. This event symbolizes the interest in demonstrating and teaching the principles of flight manifested by the Smithsonian from its inception.

Since Joseph Henry agreed in 1846 to serve as the first Secretary, there has been a harmony of endeavor between the Smithsonian Institution and those whose dream was to fly. Henry himself studied the sky and formulated a system of forecasting weather. Samuel Pierpont Langley, third Secretary of the Smithsonian, conducted experiments in flight from 1887 and on May 6, 1896, catapulted his Aerodrome No. 5 from a houseboat on the Potomac River near Quantico, Virginia. The unmanned, steam-engine driven plane with tandem staggered wings actually flew 3,300 feet and earned the distinction of being the first heavier-than-air craft to fly a significant distance.

Langley's successor, Charles Doolittle Walcott, with the support of Smithsonian Regents Ernest W. Roberts and Alexander Graham Bell (who witnessed and reported on the flights of Langley's Aerodrome No. 5), approached Congress to advocate the creation of a center for aeronautical research. In 1915, the National Advisory Committee on Aeronautics (NACA) was born. On October 1, 1958, a change of title, to the

National Aeronautics and Space Administration (NASA), reflected the widening scope of the organization.

After World War II, the chief of the U.S. Air Force, Gen. Henry Harley (Hap) Arnold, sought to preserve at least one of each of the fighter planes and bombers that the United States deployed in the war. As a result, the National Air Museum was established on August 12, 1946. At that time, Lindbergh's *Spirit of St. Louis*, the first plane to carry a solo pilot across the Atlantic Ocean, was the jewel of the Smithsonian, and it hung with other planes in the collection's home, the Arts and Industries Building. Twenty years later the National Air Museum officially became the National Air and Space Museum.

In 1976, the nation's bicentennial year, President Gerald Ford dedicated a grand, brand-new home for the museum. Architect Gyo Obata had created a monumental building of marble and glass stretching three blocks along Independence Avenue and facing the Mall. Three massive halls, two stories high, dominate the design: Milestones of Flight at the Mall entrance, Air Transportation to the right, and Space Hall on the left. Nineteen ancillary galleries, including the Langley Theater and Einstein Planetarium, augment the major exhibits.

Initially, as early as 1876, the Smithsonian's aeronautical collections began with the acquisition of a small group of Chinese kites from the Chinese Imperial Commission. But its significant gains resulted largely from the efforts of an astute and ambitious young man, Paul E. Garber, who joined the Institution in June 1920, and stayed until his death in 1992 at the age of 93.

Garber urged C.G. Abbot, Acting Secretary of the Smithsonian, to send a telegram to greet Lindbergh when he landed at Le Bourget Aerodrome near Paris on May 21, 1927. The message was congratulatory but in essence said, "We want your plane." And on April 30, 1928, the *Spirit of St. Louis* flew from its namesake city to Washington, D.C., where Charles Augustus Lindbergh presented it personally to Paul Garber of the Smithsonian.

In 1980, recognizing Garber's 60 years of service and zeal in procuring much of the museum's aeronautical collection, the Smithsonian rechristened a complex of 28 buildings housing the reserve collection of aircraft in Suitland, Maryland. Thus Paul Garber, originator of the Kite Flying Festival, was honored when Silver Hill Museum became the Paul E. Garber Preservation, Restoration and Storage Facility. Devotees of historical aircraft may tour these warehouses where planes undergo restoration. Free tours conducted by knowledgeable volunteers offer a fascinating behind-the-scenes excursion into aircraft reclamation.

The National Air and Space Museum delineates the history of aviation, from tentative attempts to fly to such technological advances as computer-controlled aircraft. It is a well-known fact that the Wright brothers' 12-second flight on December 17, 1903 marked the first successful flight of man in a heavier-than-air machine. One of the many gems of information offered by the National Air and Space Museum is the little-known fact that the Wright brothers kept flying that day at Kitty Hawk. The fourth take-off yielded a 59-second flight over a distance of 852 feet. Since that historic day, man has flown across continents and oceans, broken the sound barrier, orbited the earth, probed the galaxy and repaired a faulty telescope in outer space.

From the original Wright Flyer and Charles Lindbergh's cramped *Spirit of St. Louis*, to tiny Sputnik, the Apollo 11 command module and a Viking Mars Lander, each significant step in the evolution of aircraft, rocketry, and spacecraft is offered for study and contemplation in the Milestones of Flight gallery. Like Milestones of Flight, Air Transportation and Space Hall have a balcony vantage point for closer inspection of those artifacts that are suspended from the girders above. The Hall of Air Transportation houses the heaviest airplane in the collection – a Douglas DC-3 weighing 17,500 pounds – hanging from the ceiling. Magnificently restored in brightly painted and polished splendor, the DC-3 and other commercial aircraft illustrate progress in moving mail, passengers and cargo.

But it is in Space Hall, with its towering collection of rockets and missiles, that the sheer size of these titans dwarfs mere man. One can descend into a specially designed missile pit to gauge the scale and power required to launch a rocket or a satellite. A fast-moving queue leads to a walk through the fascinating backup model for the Skylab Orbital Workshop. Even a full-scale Hubble Telescope Test Vehicle is installed in Space Hall.

Nineteen supplementary galleries explore in depth specific areas of flight and space. One can delve into aspects of Vertical Flight, the Great War and World War II, Sea-Air Operations and Apollo to the Moon. Almost every one of these galleries has its own theater featuring short films related to its particular subject. Newest of the galleries is the popular "Where Next, Columbus?" which simulates a Martian landscape. The exhibit "The Last Act: The Atomic Bomb and the End of World War II" runs from May 1995 until January 1, 1996. Commemorating the 50th anniversary of the bombings of Hiroshima and Nagasaki, it examines the decision to use nuclear weapons and the long-term implications of the bombings.

An IMAX theater and a planetarium round out the offerings of this remarkable museum. Projected on a screen five stories high, the IMAX film "To Fly" at the Langley Theater is an unforgettable experience. From the gentle lift of a balloon as the earth falls away to a heartstopping whirl with the U.S. Navy's Blue Angels, this lyrical tribute creates the sensation of flying. "The Blue Planet" shows breath-taking views of the Earth photographed from space by astronauts, while "Destiny in Space" deals with human and robotic exploration in space. In the Einstein Planetarium, a Zeiss VI projector can create "The Stars Tonight" or explore our "Universe of Illusions" in a dazzling array of sophisticated special effects that opens up the heavens to earth-bound travellers.

MILESTONES OF FLIGHT

There it is – aloft – the Wright Flyer, the very plane that changed the course of history on December 17, 1903. Its shape is strange, the tail projecting forward ahead of the wings. It looks so breakable, yet this fragile craft of wood, fabric and wires was sturdy enough to fly and to support a man. A mannequin of Orville Wright, lying in a prone position, wears a hat, suit and tie, such conventional attire to perform such an unconventional experiment.

Lindbergh's tiny, silver monoplane with "Spirit of St. Louis" emblazoned on its nose, arrests the visitor's attention. How could a man fly across an ocean, through storms, alone, with only a compass to guide him? Lindbergh's historic flight from Roosevelt Field on Long Island, New York, began on May 20, 1927 and ended triumphantly 33 hours and 30 minutes later on May 21 at Le Bourget Aerodrome outside Paris.

Still "flying high" overhead is the jaunty persimmon-colored Bell X-1, the plane that broke the sound barrier in 1947. Its needle-nose points towards the rocket-powered X-15, which flew to Mach 6 (six times the speed of sound) only 12 years later.

Dramatically representing progress in rocketry, a full-scale model of Robert H. Goddard's first rocket to use liquid propellant successfully on March 16, 1926, stands next to the scientist's most advanced rocket. In 1926, the rocket shot up about 40 feet in a flight lasting less than three seconds. By 1941, Goddard had developed a rocket which combined most of the components used in today's long-range rockets and boosters into space.

On October 4, 1957, the Union of Soviet Socialist Republics stunned the world by blasting an artificial satellite into orbit around the Earth. Sputnik, meaning "fellow traveler", launched a fierce competition to control outer space. About the size of a beach ball, the replica of Sputnik I is easy to miss. The best vantage point for this and other satellites is from the overlook on the second floor.

The United States Space Program is represented by the Mercury spacecraft *Friendship 7*, flown by John Glenn, who became the first American to orbit the Earth on February 20, 1962. The Gemini program sent two men into space. Hatch open, Gemini 4 reproduces the initial moment of Edward H. White's walk in space on June 3, 1965.

On July 20, 1969, two Americans became the first men to land on the moon. Columbia, the Apollo 11 command module that safely returned to Earth the three astronauts on the mission, enjoys prominent display, its original heat shield scorched but intact. Also among the Milestones are moon rocks. One of the delights of this area is to be able to run one's fingers over smooth, black basaltic lunar rock.

At the dedication of the museum in 1976, no one would have predicted the treaty reduction of Soviet and American missiles. Standing side by side, Pershing II and SS-20 are just two representatives of more than 2,600 nuclear missiles eliminated by the Intermediate-range Nuclear Forces Treaty in December 1987.

The Viking I Lander alighted on Mars July 20, 1976 and returned spectacular photos and data to Earth periodically until 1982. The almost identical lander on display reminds us that the National Air and Space Museum will have to make room for future milestones of flight.

11 Every year millions of school children, foreign visitors and American tourists create a pleasant hubbub as they flood the entrance to the museum. Three exhibits commemorate firsts in aeronautic history: the first flight, breaking the sound barrier, and returning men safely from the moon.

12/13 Four years of experiments preceded the creation of the Wright Flyer. They included constructing a wind-tunnel, over 1,000 glider flights, and the invention that made the flight successful: wing-warping. On December 17, 1903, it was Orville's turn as pilot and the wind at Kill Devil Hill, North Carolina, blew a steady 21 mph. He made history that day as the first man to fly in a heavier-than-air craft. Precisely 45 years later, the Wright Flyer was hung at the entrance to the Arts and Industries Building of the Smithsonian Institution. Now, with the figure of Orville as pilot, it commands a place of honor in the National Air and Space Museum.

14 In 1919, Raymond Orteig offered a $25,000 prize for the first nonstop flight between Paris and New York City. Competition was fierce. Former barnstormer and mail pilot Charles A. Lindbergh persuaded a group of St. Louis businessmen to fund his Ryan NYP (New York to Paris) monoplane. In his 1953 Pulitzer Prize winning book The Spirit of St. Louis, Lindbergh describes dropping 50 feet above the waves and shouting to a fisherman, "Which way is Ireland?" He got no answer. He found Ireland, then Paris, where a throng of delirious Parisians welcomed him.

15 Upon Lindbergh's triumphant return to the United States, the nation's capital and New York City greeted him with tumultuous welcome. Then he flew the Spirit of St. Louis across the country as a kind of aerial good-will ambassador and landed in major cities. Flags painted on the forward fuselage represent countries he visited in the Western Hemisphere.

16 In 1919, Robert Hutchings Goddard wrote a treatise, "A Method of Reaching Extreme Altitudes," in which he envisioned rocketing to the moon. The slender Goddard rocket at left was fired in 1926, the first liquid fuel rocket. The 1941 rocket on the right towers over its predecessor, dramatically illustrating Goddard's advanced designs in rocketry.

17 Poised as though to blast through the glass ceiling, the Soviet missile SS-20 and the U.S. Army Pershing II represent two powerful nuclear missiles of over 2,600 banned by the 1987 Intermediate-range Nuclear Forces Treaty (INF) between the United States and the Soviet Union.

18/19 Sleek and beautiful, the North American
X-15 hypersonic research aircraft pioneered
development of aerodynamic design,
advanced materials, and rocket propulsion in
preparation for space flight. The X-15's
experimental flights soared higher in 1963
(over 67 miles up) and faster in 1967 (over
4,000 mph) than any other airplane in history.
The rocket-propelled machine was the first to
fly four, five, and six times the speed of sound
(Mach 4, Mach 5, and Mach 6).

20 On October 14, 1947, Captain Charles
''Chuck'' Yeager piloted this distinctive
apricot-colored plane into aviation history.
Glamorous Glennis, named for Yeager's wife,
proved it was possible to fly faster than sound.
Launched from a Boeing B-29 over
California's Mojave Desert, the Bell X-1
achieved the first supersonic flight.

21 Caught in earthly sunlight, this artificial
satellite is a replica of Mariner 2. Launched on
December 14, 1962, Mariner 2 flew 109 days
to within 21,600 miles of Venus, and reported
to Earth, 36 million miles away, that the
temperature of our nearest neighbor was
about 800° F

22 On February 20, 1962 John Glenn, the first
American sent into orbit, made three
revolutions of the Earth in four hours and 55
minutes. By removing a portion of the Mercury
capsule, the museum shows the position of
the astronaut in Friendship 7.

23 In the Gemini 4 spacecraft are two figures
representing James McDivitt at the controls
and Edward H. White II emerging from the
capsule to become the first American to walk
in space. Tethered to the capsule, he
demonstrated that astronauts could work and
maneuver in space.

24/25 Standing proudly in the center of The Space Mural: A Cosmic View, is the Apollo astronaut planting an American flag on the moon. Robert McCall's 75-foot-wide painting on the east wall of Independence Avenue Lobby begins with Earth's explosive creation and climaxes in a vertical section leaping into distant galaxies.

26 From December 14 to December 23, 1986, Dick Rutan and Jeana Yeager piloted this experimental aircraft from Edwards Air Force Base, California, nonstop and non-refueled around the world, returning to Edwards Air Force Base. Designed by Burt Rutan, this graceful craft now hovers over the Information Desk.

27 Possibly the most aesthetic flying fuel tank ever built, Voyager averaged 115.65 mph and swept in a great circle of 24,986.727 miles in just over 9 days to set a world record ''without a pit stop.''

28/29 This 185-pound sphere with antennae is a replica of Sputnik I, the first artificial satellite to orbit the Earth. Launched in Russia on October 4, 1957, Sputnik took 95 minutes to circle the Earth, and for 21 days transmitted battery-powered radio signals.

28

30 It took 10 months for a Viking Lander identical to this reproduction to reach Mars. Launched March 20, 1975, it alighted on the following July 20, 1976 and transmitted photos and other data to Earth periodically until November 1982.

31 The very definition of Milestones of Air and Space is exemplified by the position of Pioneer 10 between the Spirit of St. Louis and tiny Sputnik I. This spin-stabilized spacecraft was launched March 3, 1972, to explore the outer planets of our solar system. By December 3, 1973, it passed within 82,000 miles of Jupiter, returning its scientific data to Earth.

32/33 Alejandro Otero's striking sculpture, Delta Solar, constantly shifts its steel sails in response to ambient breezes. Located on Independence Avenue at the 7th Street side of the museum, the delightful mobile was a bicentennial gift to the people of the United States from the government of Venezuela.

SPACE HALL

Space Hall is one vast stage for props in the theater of space. In this cavernous gallery, three mammoth exhibits dominate. Towering in one corner is the backup for the Skylab Orbital Workshop, one of a cluster of huge vehicles that include the Airlock Module and the Multiple Docking Adapter. Elevated toward the glass wall is the Apollo-Soyuz Test Project. The newest installation is a full-scale Hubble Telescope Test Vehicle.

Skylab provided a complete environment for astronauts to live and work in space for extended periods. Designed for eight months of service, the unmanned, 199,750-pound cluster of Skylab vehicles was launched on May 14, 1973. The first of its three three-man crews docked 11 days later in an Apollo Command Module and remained for 28 days, conducting scientific experiments. A second crew spent almost two months in space and the third, 84 days. In July 1979, debris from Skylab plummeted to Earth and some parts were recovered from the Australian desert.

One of the primary purposes of the mission was to study the effects of prolonged weightlessness on the astronauts. The tour passes through the crew's quarters which contain areas for preparing food, dining, washing, and waste disposal – there's even a stationary bicycle for exercise. The wardroom contained Skylab's only sizable window. The Orbital Workshop portion is a mind-boggling 48 feet long and weighs 80,000 pounds.

Two other elements of the Skylab cluster are displayed here. The Multiple Docking Adapter lies on its side. Through this long cylinder the astronaut passed into the Airlock Module, designed to protect the temperature and atmosphere of Skylab. From there, the astronaut could exit the lab for a space walk. For exhibit, one section of its external shell has been removed to expose its components, a maze of cables, wires and connections.

The progenitor of international cooperation in space exploration was the Apollo-Soyuz Test Project. Stretching completely across the front of Space Hall is the union of two dissimilar spacecraft: one gleaming silver cylinder labeled "United States", the other an apple-green oversized "egg-cup" lettered in red, CCCP, initials in the Russian alphabet for Soyuz Sovetskikh Sotsialisticheskikh Respublik (U.S.S.R.). This strange marriage in outer space, symbolic of detente, took place on July 17, 1975, after three years of preparation. For two days after their historic handshake, three astronauts and two cosmonauts conducted experiments and "broke bread" together.

The Hubble Space Telescope, the largest ever built, was launched in 1990. However, it was an embarrassment to the European Space Agency and NASA, its joint sponsors. Although it was designed to function for 15 years, a defect in the mirror of the main optical system severely limited its range. In December 1993, a special mission accomplished the repair. In July 1994, Hubble redeemed itself by returning dramatic, sharp images of fragments of the Shoemaker-Levy 9 comet crashing into Jupiter.

35 A descent into the specially designed missile pit in Space Hall forces neck-aching appreciation of the rocket size required to blast warheads to a distant target, or sounding rockets with scientific instruments and launch vehicles for spacecraft.

36/37 Visitors on the midpoint viewing platform dramatize the size of the cluster of missiles in the center. Suspended at right is the Northrop/NASA-designed M2-F3 ''Lifting Body,'' an experimental wingless aircraft that made 16 flights between July 1966 and May 1967. Rebuilt after a crash, it was retired in late 1972.

38 The line to enter Skylab appears to be formidable, but it moves quickly. It is worth a momentary delay to walk through the backup of the Skylab Orbital Workshop and inspect the living quarters of men who lived for as long as nearly three months in space.

39 top Literally exhibiting the nuts and bolts of engineering, the museum has removed a portion of the shell of Skylab's Airlock Module, through which the astronaut passed before drifting out to ''walk'' in space.

39 bottom Astronauts on Skylab collected scientific data using visible and infrared light in a technique called multispectral scanning. Their findings helped to detect insect infestation, map deserts, calculate ice and snow cover, locate mineral deposits, and track migrations of marine life and wildlife. In the wardroom display, an unopened can floats above the astronaut's right hand as he copes with having lunch in space.

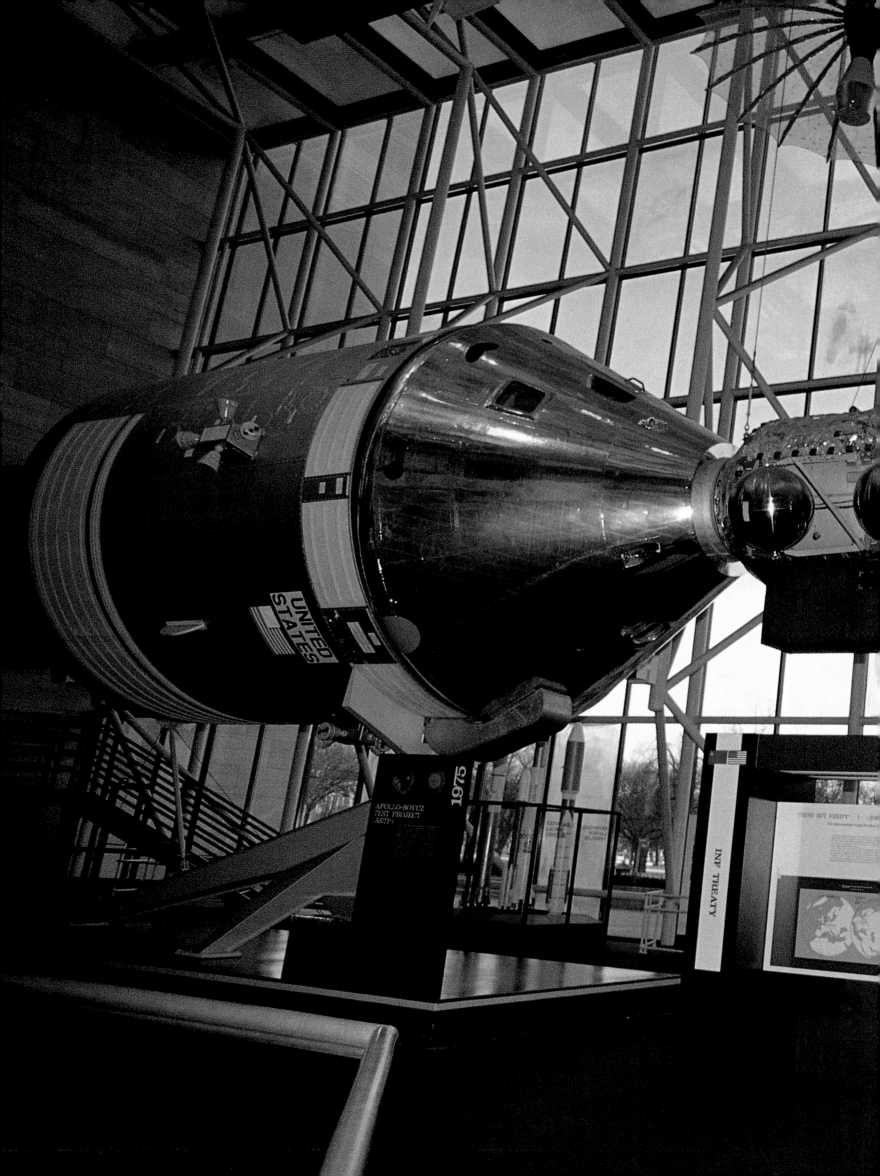

40/41 A rendezvous in space, the Apollo-Soyuz Test Project, stretches across Space Hall. Apollo carried the Docking Adapter that allowed the link-up on July 17, 1975, between two Russian cosmonauts in the apple-green craft and three American astronauts in the cone-shaped Apollo Command Module.

42 Launched two days earlier, Soyuz linked up to Apollo 140 miles above the Atlantic Ocean in the first international mission to use outer space for peaceful purposes.

43 This unique perspective shows the exhaust cone for the main propulsion system in the cylindrical Apollo Service Module.

44 In December 1993, people watched TV in fascination as astronauts on a special mission of the space shuttle Endeavour accomplished the repair of the Hubble Space Telescope's main optical system. Endeavour traveled 365 miles from the launch to make the necessary adjustments. On exhibit is the Hubble Structural Dynamic Test Vehicle, which resembles the actual flight vehicle.

45 Hugging the ceiling of glass is a full-scale model of a Tracking and Data Relay Satellite (TDRS), the system designed for locating a spacecraft and commanding it to complete specific tasks. The translucent umbrellas are antennae, and the rectangular solar arrays are held by a single arm.

46 Comparatively small, this German V-1
guided missile was developed for use in World
War II. Nearly 25 feet in length, it was packed
with almost a ton of explosives in its warhead.
To Germans, it was Vengeance Weapon One,
but to the British, who were targets, it was
"The Buzz Bomb," because a pulsing jet
engine broadcast its approach.

47 Thrusting its powerful body just over 60
feet from the floor of the missile pit is the U.S.
Minuteman III, an intercontinental ballistic
missile (ICBM). Its preset guidance system
can direct the strategic missile to a target as
far as 8,000 miles away.

48/49 "The Eagle has landed," came the
message on July 20, 1969, from Tranquility
Base on the moon. In the east gallery just
outside the cafeteria, this Apollo Lunar Module
backup reproduces that historic touchdown.

50 The Lunar Module carried astronauts from
Apollo 11 Command Module to and from the
moon. Models of Commander Neil A.
Armstrong (left) and LM Pilot Edwin E. "Buzz"
Aldrin, Jr. display the special life-support
systems they wore for their historic
explorations on the moon.

51 Used for the first time on April 12, 1981,
space shuttles flew two to nine missions every
year except in 1986 and 1987. This 1:15 scale
model shows the orbiter, main engines,
external tank, and solid rocket boosters. The
actual orbiter is 122 feet tall, with a 78-foot
wingspan and speed of 17,300 mph.

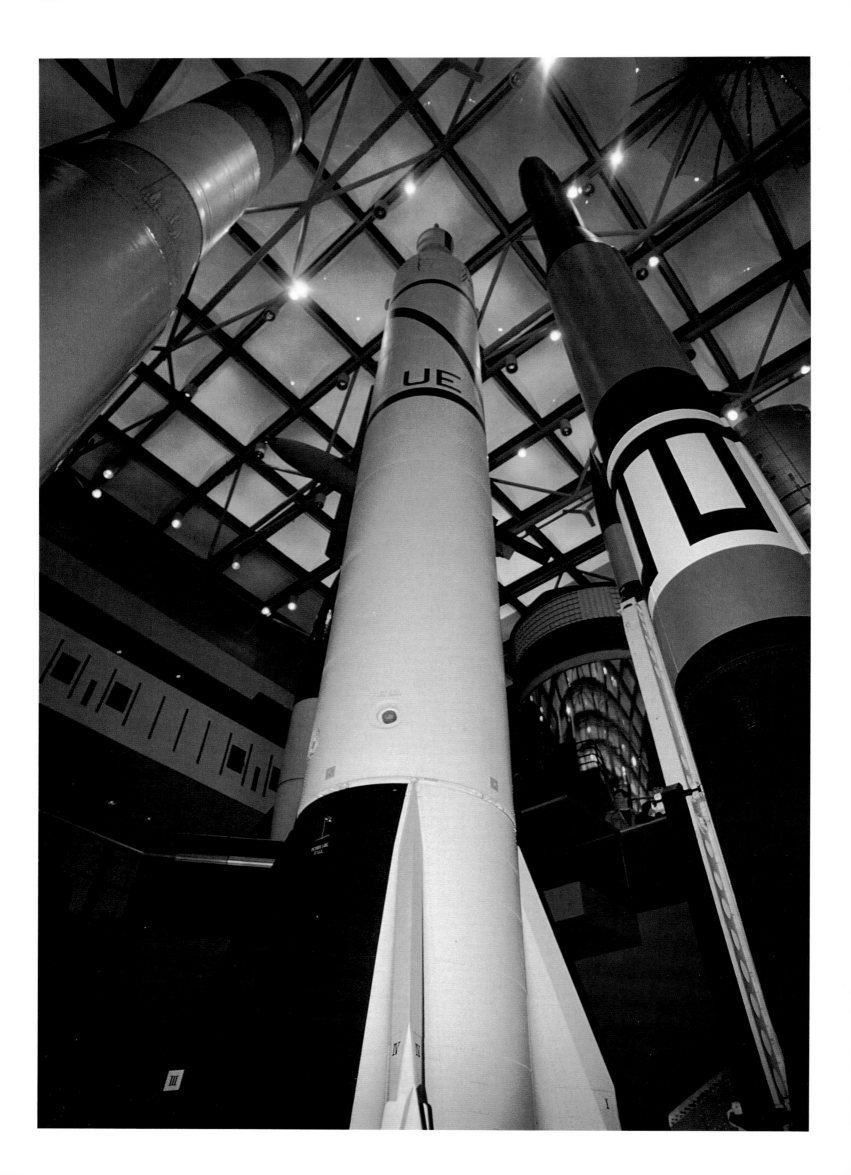

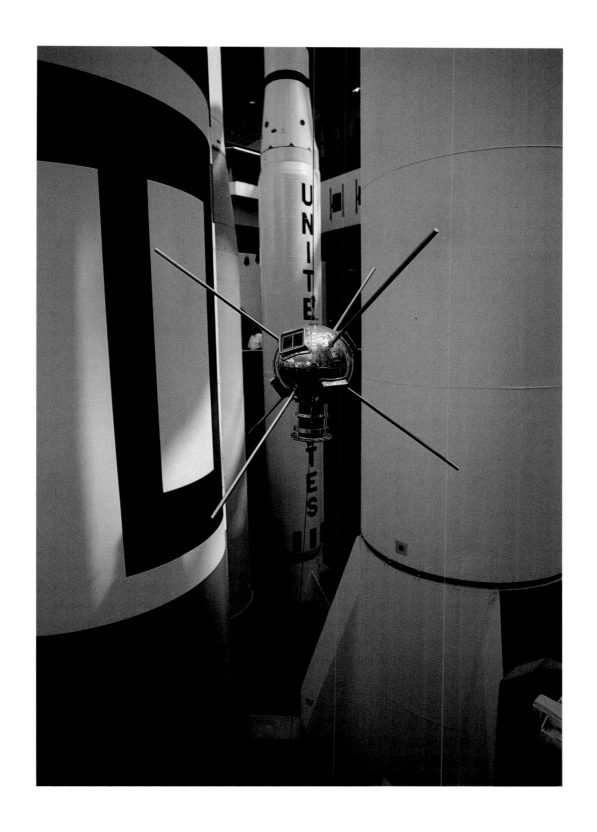

52 Jupiter C, bearing the letters UE, is a
modified Redstone ballistic missile, the type
Wernher von Braun used on January 31, 1958
to place Explorer I into orbit. It was America's
answer to Sputnik. The Minuteman III ICBM
stands to the left and the Vanguard launch to
the right of the viewer.

53 It took the behemoth three-stage
Vanguard rocket on the left to launch the tiny
50-pound Vanguard I satellite, at center, into
orbit. The U.S. satellite participated in the
observation of the International Geophysical
Year, 1958. In the background is the Scout D,
a four-stage solid propellant satellite launch
vehicle.

AIR TRANSPORTATION

The Hall of Air Transportation salutes airplanes. Led by the Pitcairn Mailwing, the fleet of planes hanging from the ceiling illustrates the history of transport, from biplanes delivering mail, through open cockpit mail/passenger planes, to the dependable Douglas DC-3. Even those exhibited on the floor seem ready for take-off.

Lindbergh's transatlantic success in May 1927 stimulated interest in commercial flight. But as early as 1918, airplanes regularly carried mail between Washington D.C., Philadelphia and New York City. By 1926, mail routes were established between Los Angeles and Salt Lake City in the West and between New York City and Atlanta in the East. Lindbergh himself was one of three mail pilots shuttling between St. Louis and Chicago.

Even Henry Ford was convinced of the viability of the airplane, and made a brief foray into supervising aircraft design and construction in the late 1920s and early 1930s. The famous Ford Tri-motor, nicknamed the "Tin Goose", is one of the aircraft suspended from the girders in the Hall.

Almost eclipsed by larger planes in its wake, the single engine Northrop Alpha in the center of the formation provided the transition between pioneer and modern passenger service. While the pilot sat in an open cockpit, six passengers were accommodated in an enclosed cabin. Behind the Alpha, in perpetual static chase are two significant developments in passenger service: Boeing's 1930 Model 247 which carried 10 people, and the airplane that made passenger service profitable for the first time, the Douglas DC-3 with space for 21 to 28 aboard.

Like a giant black and yellow bumble-bee, the twin-engine Grumman Goose Amphibian perches on the floor and confidently displays its slogan, "Commuting in the Modern Manner." Its deep fuselage could serve as a hull, making it extremely adaptable. A crew of two could fly up to six businessmen from estates on Long Island, New York, to offices in downtown Manhattan.

Most people who visit the museum have probably flown in a plane. Consequently Air Transportation is the section most directly related to their experience. Encouraging close-up inspection, the museum has taken the nose section from a Douglas DC-7, the American Airlines Flagship *Vermont*, and allowed tourists to walk up the gangway, peer into the cockpit and stroll through the passenger section to see what accommodations offered in the late 1950s looked like.

55 In the Hall of Air Transportation, the planes appear to fly through the air with the greatest of ease. By suspending them all heading in the same direction, the museum graphically traces the development of commercial air travel from biplane to the beginning of modern air transport, as typified by the Douglas DC-3.

56/57 From the second floor of this two-story
hall, one can almost feel the Ford Tri-motor
flying overhead. This photograph captures the
pageant of aviation history.

58/59 This spunky little Pitcairn Mailwing seems to be buzzing the National Gallery of Art, across the Mall. A reliable aircraft, the PA-5 flew mail routes to Texas in 1927 and on the east coast in 1928. When it became obsolete, the sturdy plane was used as a crop-duster. Eastern Air Transport is better known today as Eastern Air Lines.

PITCAIRN
MAILWING

60 In this exhibit, as the pilot slips into the
open cockpit, sacks of mail are stuffed into a
Douglas M-2. Behind it is one of the flashing
beacons placed at 10-mile intervals on major
mail routes to facilitate night flights. One of the
first airmail planes, this M-2 served the Los
Angeles to Salt Lake City route from 1926 to
1930.

61 A practical man, Henry Ford foresaw the potential of air transport. This handsome Ford 5-AT Tri-motor, affectionately called the "Tin Goose" because of its corrugated aluminum body, was in production from 1926 to 1933.

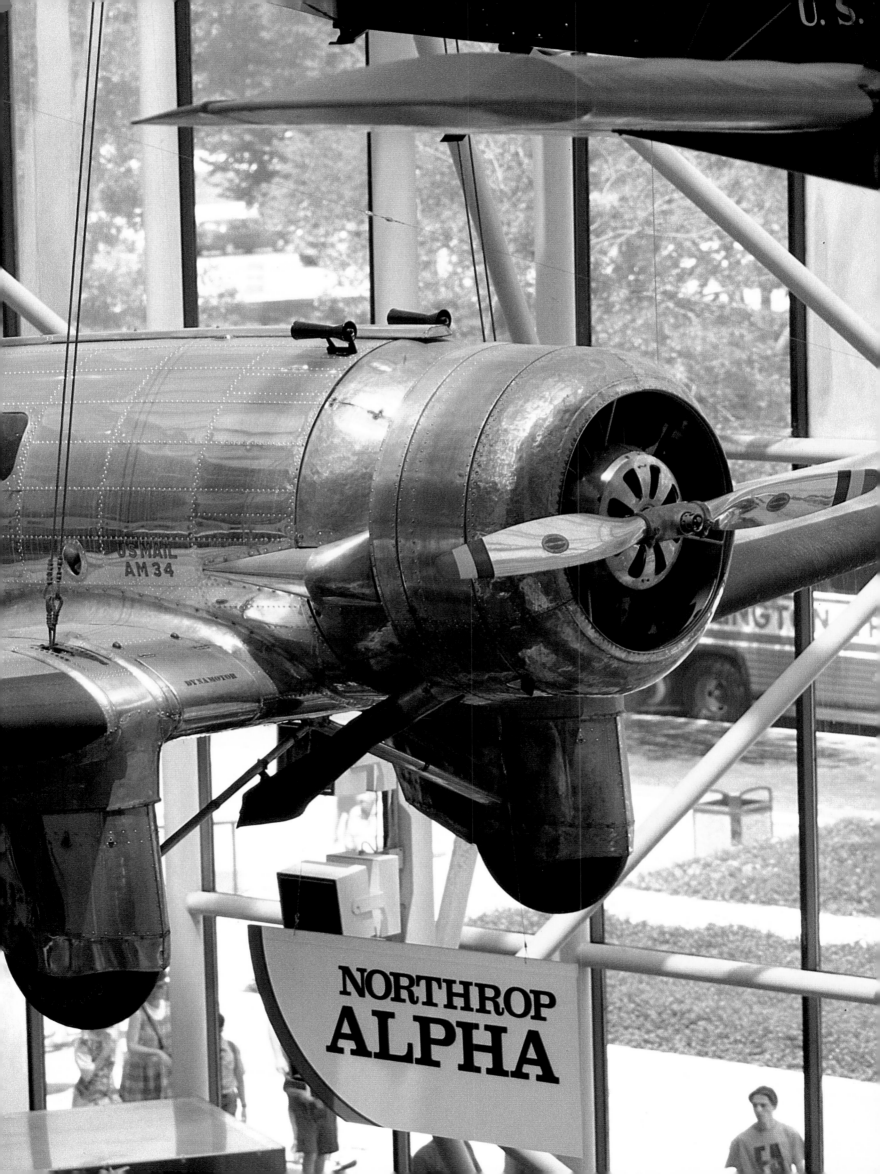

NORTHROP
ALPHA

62/63 Strategically placed in the center of the fleet of planes, the gleaming Northrop Alpha shows the early streamlining in airplane design. Although the pilot was exposed to the elements, six passengers traveled in relative comfort. The Alpha could cross the country in 23 hours at its top speed of 177 mph.

64 Under the protective wing of the Douglas DC-3 perches the black and yellow twin-engine Grumman Goose Amphibian. In the Air Transportation hall there are six suspended aircraft, two on the floor, and the entire nose section of a Douglas DC-7.

65 The flashy Grumman G-21 "Goose," designed for the private and commercial market, first flew in June 1937. Its deep hull and floats under the wing transformed it to a seaplane. It has proven so versatile that amphibians like this are still in use today.

66 Seated before a control panel, a robot demonstrates the General Electric CF 6 Turbofan Engine. As the robot slowly pushes the throttle forward, one can hear and see the engine rev. After World War II, gas turbines (or ''jet'' engines) gradually replaced piston engines. Turbines were not only more powerful and much lighter, they were also mechanically simpler.

67 One can easily imagine the roar of engines overhead in the Hall of Air Transportation. In the background, the Air Traffic Control exhibit salutes pilots, stewards and stewardesses who serve the flying public. Visitors line up to board the forward fuselage of the American Airlines DC-7 Flagship Vermont.

68/69 Suspended behind the Ford Tri-motor is one of the most remarkable airplanes in the world, the Douglas DC-3. Originally designed in the mid-1930s to afford sleeper berths for transcontinental commercial flights, this reliable aircraft (military designation C-47) was used to transport Allied supplies and troops in World War II.

DOUGLAS
DC 3

BORN TO FLY

When she was 10 years old in the early 1960s, Patty Wagstaff blithely informed her parents that she was going to be a pilot. In 1980, she obtained her private pilot's license in Alaska. Wagstaff pursued her calling, eventually becoming an instructor in multi-engine craft and competing in aerobatics. She won the United States National Aerobatic Championship in 1991, 1992, and 1993, and placed second to Phil Knight in 1994. In the Pioneers of Flight gallery, she joins legendary individuals and the planes they flew into the record books.

Most of the heralded individual pilots can be found there. However, heroes and heroines in the epic of flight are featured in the Blacks in Aviation section of Pioneers in Flight, as well as in other galleries: Early Flight, Golden Age of Flight, Vertical Flight, and particularly Flight Testing.

The roster of aviation greats is studded with long-esteemed names: Glenn Curtiss, Charles Lindbergh, Jimmy Doolittle, Amelia Earhart, Howard Hughes and Wiley Post. In every case, the actual planes they flew are on display. Among them is Amelia Earhart's crayon-red Lockheed Vega, which Jimmy Doolittle described as "every kid's idea of what an airplane ought to look like."

Some bright flames flared, then sputtered out. Otto Lilienthal, the original hang-glider, went soaring in 1894, but two years later he died from injuries when his glider stalled. Dare-devil Calbraith Perry Rodgers was an early high-flying advertiser. In 1911, he tried to win the lordly sum of $50,000 offered by William Randolph Hearst to the aviator who flew across the United States in 30 days. The plucky pilot, flying a canvas-covered Wright EX biplane, didn't win the prize. But in 70 landings, the decorated plane certainly did justice to his sponsor, the Armour Company, promoting its Vin Fiz grape soft drink. Four months later he lost his life in a crash in the Pacific.

In 1912 Harriet Quimby became the first woman to fly solo across the English Channel. Svelte and stylish, Quimby wore a plum satin flying outfit. Months after the Channel crossing, she fell from her airplane to her death. American Bessie Coleman was a stunt pilot. In that era, blacks who were born to fly had to travel to France to become licensed pilots. Coleman did, returned to the United States, and after her accidental death, became an inspiration to other black aviators.

Most fliers like H. Ross Perot, Jr. and Jay Coburn live to enjoy their success. On September 30, 1982, they alighted in Forth Worth, Texas, in the *Spirit of Texas*. In just over 29 days, the two men had been the first to circumnavigate the world in a helicopter.

Most of the supplementary galleries have intimate theaters featuring brief, repeated films. These presentations are outstanding documentaries. In the Flight Testing gallery, "The Aeroplane: A Chronicle of Flight in Moving Pictures" includes actual footage of the airborne 1909 Wright Military Flyer, as well as many early-bird contraptions.

71 One of the most celebrated pilots in the world, Amelia Earhart, stepped up to this saucy Lockheed Vega intent on setting records for long-distance solo flights by a woman. She did, spanning the Atlantic in May 1932, and making the first transcontinental flight by a woman from Los Angeles to Newark in 19 hours, 5 minutes, August 24-25, 1932.

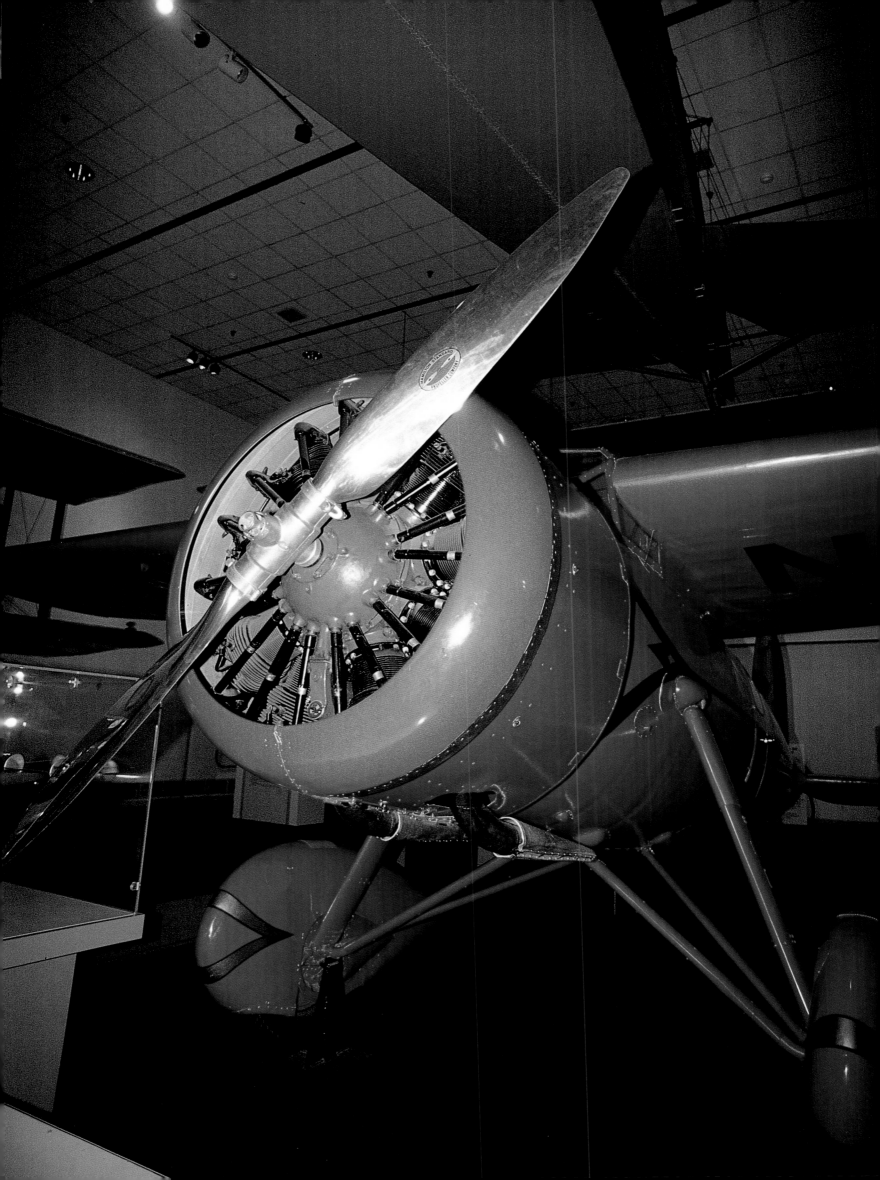

72 top In this insignia, American eagles flying around the world for the U.S. Army Air Service symbolize the purpose of four Douglas World Cruisers in the first successful attempt to encircle the globe. The Chicago *was the second of four.*

72 bottom On April 6, 1924, the Chicago, Seattle, Boston *and* New Orleans, *each with a two-man crew in the open cockpit biplane, left Seattle, Washington. On September 28, 175 days later, two of the original four, plus a substitute* Boston, *landed in Seattle. The Douglas World Cruiser averaged 70 mph on a harrowing round-the-world flight.*

73 Exactly five years after Lindbergh's conquest of the Atlantic Ocean, Amelia Earhart became the first woman to solo nonstop across the Atlantic, from Newfoundland to Northern Ireland, May 20-21, 1932. She completed the transatlantic crossing in 14 hours, 54 minutes in this sporty Lockheed 5-B Vega designed by John Northrop.

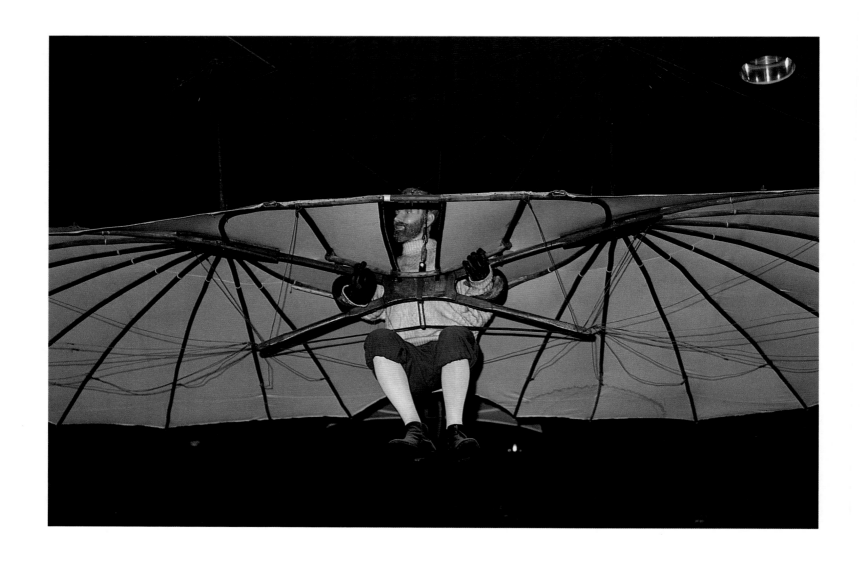

74 Like a giant moth, the figure of German
aeronautical experimenter Otto Lilienthal
hovers near the entrance to the gallery of Early
Flight. In this 1894 glider constructed of
bamboo and willow covered with cotton cloth,
Lilienthal, supported by a criss-cross of bars
under his arms, controlled the glider by
moving his body, particularly the legs.

75 New York's aviation pioneer, Glenn Curtiss, designed this 1912 "Headless Pusher." Famed stunt pilot Lincoln Beachey sat in the seat and propped his feet on either side of the front wheel, with the four-cylinder pusher engine behind him. Beachey actually did loops and dives in this during exhibition flying.

76/77 In this boxy Fokker T-2 monoplane with a wingspan of almost 80 feet, Lts. Oakley G. Kelly and John A. Macready made the first successful coast to coast flight. It took 26 hours, 50 minutes to fly from Roosevelt Field, Long Island, New York, to Rockwell Field, San Diego, California, on May 2 and 3, 1922.

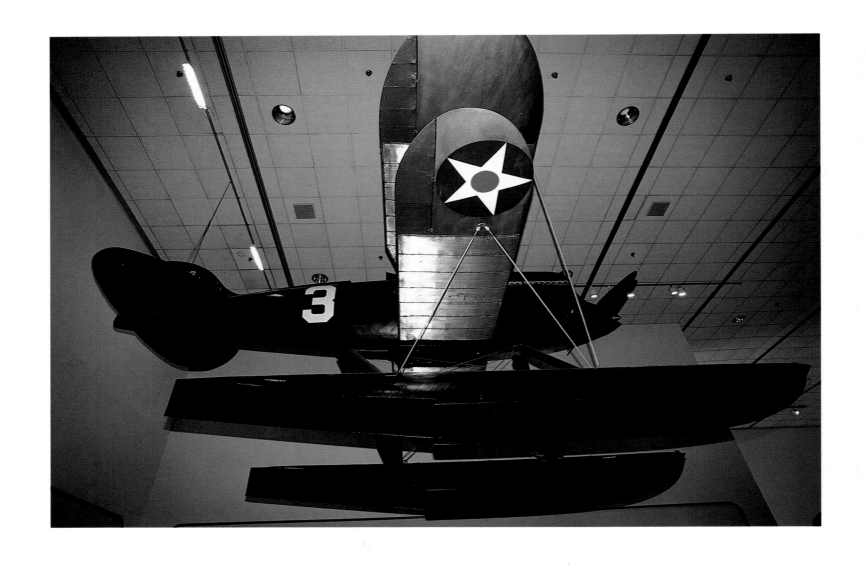

78 As early as 1911, Glenn Curtiss had used
ailerons and attached them to his seaplane.
By 1925, this Curtiss R3C-2 boasted a 600-
horsepower engine. U.S. Army Lt. J.H.
''Jimmy'' Doolittle flew this beauty to victory in
the 1925 Schneider Trophy Race for
seaplanes, averaging 232 mph.

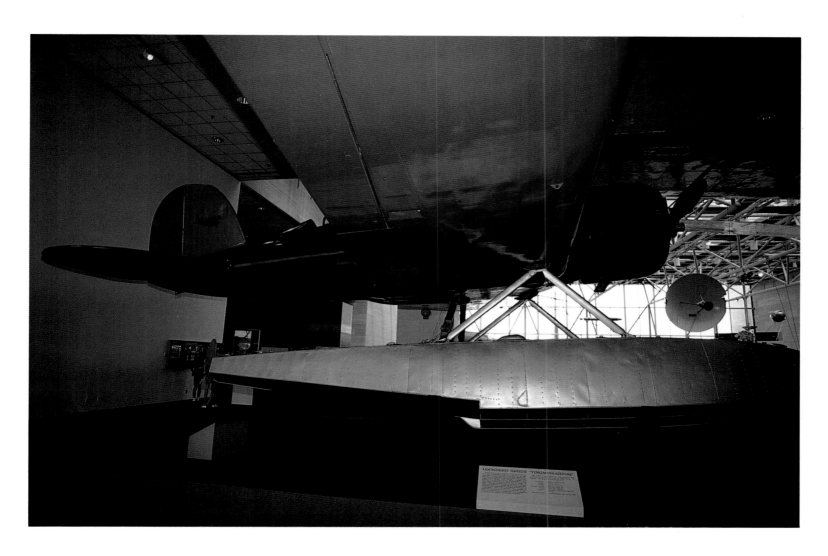

79 top Lindbergh met his wife, Anne Morrow, when he flew the Spirit of St. Louis to Mexico on a good-will tour. She was the U.S. ambassador's daughter. After their marriage in 1929, he taught her to fly. Together in 1931 they flew this two-seater, open cockpit Lockheed 8 Sirius, outfitted with special pontoons, to the Orient. Two years later the Lindberghs developed Pan American air routes in this plane.

79 bottom Neatly lettered on the fuselage, Tingmissartoq means, "The man who flies like a big bird." An Eskimo boy in Greenland had found one word in his language that described Charles Lindbergh so appropriately.

80 Airplanes have been adapted to any
conditions. Here's one with skiis. Explorer
Lincoln Ellsworth and pilot Herbert Hollick-
Kenyon flew successfully across Antarctica
late in 1935 in the sturdy Northrop Gamma 2B
Polar Star *which had controls in both
cockpits.*

81 Howard Hughes designed this sleek low-winged monoplane for one purpose: to set a world record for speed, which he did in September 1935, reaching 352 mph. The H-1 Racer is a triumph of aerodynamic design and classic beauty.

82 top This snappy midget racer is about the
size of a pick-up truck with wings. The
Wittman Buster's length is about 17½ feet,
and its wingspan only 15 feet. But it could,
and did, win races or finish near the top from
1947 to its retirement in 1954.

82 bottom Wiley Post made Winnie Mae
famous. In this dependable Lockheed 5-C
Vega, Post made two round-the-world record-
setting flights. He also took Winnie Mae up to
50,000 feet to test a pressurized suit he had
invented to enable pilots to fly in the sub-
stratosphere.

83 The flying suit belongs to diminutive Patty
Wagstaff, winner of the U.S. National
Aerobatic Championships in 1991, '92, and
'93. She won her first two national titles in this
trim Extra 260, designed by Walter Extra. A
video showing the rigors of aerobatics
includes Wagstaff executing her trademark
maneuver: a series of snap rolls in a perfect
360° circle.

84/85 Featherweight materials and a champion bicyclist made manpowered flight possible. Drs. Paul Macready and Peter Lissamen used mylar, tubular aluminum, stainless steel, cardboard, and styrofoam to create the Gossamer Condor. On August 23, 1977, Bryan Allen pedalled furiously to lift the Condor over 10 feet and complete a figure-eight over a half-mile course in 7 minutes, 27 seconds. The team won $95,000.

86 Equipment and parachutes are dangling outside the National Geographic/U.S. Army gondola. Funded by the National Geographic Society, the balloon was filled with nonflammable helium. The gondola is constructed of welded magnesium and aluminum alloy sections. Launched November 11, 1935 in Rapid City, South Dakota, Explorer II carried two aeronauts plus instruments to a world record altitude of 72,395 feet.

87 This Bell 206L-1 LongRanger II helicopter
carried Jay Coburn and H. Ross Perot, Jr. to a
world record for a helicopter flight around the
globe. It took just over 29 days from
September 1 to September 30, 1982. The
Spirit of Texas which began and ended its
adventure in Fort Worth, Texas, is displayed in
the Vertical Flight gallery.

MILITARY USE OF AIRCRAFT

In December 1907, the Signal Corps drew up specifications for a heavier-than-air flying machine, and announced it would accept sealed bids for the U.S. Army. The Wright brothers set out to design a plane that would meet those requirements. After an accident took the life of Lt. Thomas O. Selfridge, a second biplane was built and tested. In 1909, the Signal Corps accepted the Wright Military Flyer and paid its builders $30,000 for the first military aircraft in the world. It is on display in the gallery of Early Flight.

Early in World War I, planes were used for scouting positions of the enemy. But in 1915, Dutch engineer Anthony Herman Gerard Fokker, a builder of planes, also developed a machine gun that was synchronized to shoot through revolving propeller blades. The airplane became a weapon.

The National Air and Space Museum's World War I gallery is entitled Legend, Memory and the Great War in the Air. Just beyond the entrance, a red-and-white-checkered biplane soars over a theater marquee. "Hollywood Knights of the Sky" features continuous showing of scenes from great melodramas of the era, such as *Ace of Aces* and *Hell's Angels.* Within the gallery, elaborate lifesize dioramas recreate a German aircraft factory, an unexploded Zeppelin bomb in London, and an aerial skirmish with sound effects.

In the World War II Aviation gallery, artist Keith Ferris' panoramic mural of the Boeing B-17G, *Thunderbird,* on a bombing raid to Wiesbaden, Germany, provides a dramatic background for World War II fighters. The best-known fighters from five countries are here: an American Mustang P-51D lettered *Willit Run*?, Germany's Messerschmitt Bf 109, Britain's Spitfire, Japan's Zero, and Italy's Macchi C.202, dabbed with camouflage for desert aerial combat.

A Martin B-26 Marauder, a survivor of the European Theater, has a bomb painted on it for each of its 202 missions. Although only the nose section is exhibited, aptly-named *Flak Bait* had over 1,000 patches on it at the end of the war.

An outstanding collection of World War II memorabilia includes one of Bill Mauldin's sardonic "Willy and Joe" cartoons, an issue of *Stars and Stripes,* and photos of pin-up queens Betty Grable, Rita Hayworth and Veronica Lake. In the theater, William Wyler's documentary of the B-17 *Memphis Belle* has been reduced from 41 to 18 minutes of graphic scenes of aerial combat. The first jet-propelled warplane used in combat during World War II, the Messerschmitt Me 262, is featured in the Jet Aviation gallery.

Sea-Air Operations gallery is an effectively simulated aircraft carrier experience aboard the museum's own USS *Smithsonian.* From the hangar deck's verisimilitude, with intercoms, ladders and ship's lockers on battleship-grey walls to its sounds and sights of other ships passing by, one feels truly aboard a carrier. But it is Prifly, the ship's traffic control tower, where the excitement is. Simulated by film and sound effects, 20-ton jets appear to land and take off from the flight deck.

The gallery Beyond the Limits addresses the revolutionary impact of the computer on flight technology. In the past 20 years, as computers grew in power, they shrank in size. To illustrate this graphically, a glass pillar contains a million transistors surrounding a single computer chip. They are equal in power.

Computer technology has altered basic aerodynamic design and almost taken over for the pilot. Suspended in the gallery, a full-scale model of the military aircraft of the future, a 1984 experimental Grumman X-29 has radically designed wings that sweep forward and three on-board computers that operate the controls to keep it stable so the pilot can maneuver the plane.

89 At the west end of the museum, the
flamboyant orange biplane, a Grumman G-22
Gulfhawk II, flies in formation with two other
pre-World War II fighters: a Boeing P-26A
Peashooter at center, and a Curtiss P-40
Warhawk. The P-40 went on to be flown by
the Flying Tigers in China, and during WWII by
the U.S. and its allies.

90/91 Although the Wright Military Flyer of
1909 satisfied Signal Corps specifications for
carrying two people, it is exhibited here with
only the figure of the pilot. The wings, two
propellers and the engine were behind the
aviator. This first military aircraft in the world
could remain airborne over an hour and cover
42 miles.

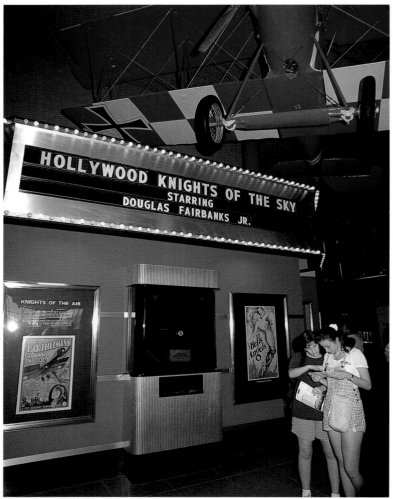

92 top Poised to fire down on the enemy, this mustached pilot in the fur coat is as menacing as the bat-like logo on this French World War I bomber, a Voisin VIII. Built for reconnaissance, by 1916 Voisins were bombing German factories and attempting night raids.

92 bottom Only in Hollywood would this World War I German fighter, a Pfalz D.XII, be painted like a checkerboard. Soaring over the marquee of the theater, this is how the plane appeared in the 1930 Hollywood classic, Dawn Patrol.

93 The museum's Looking at Earth gallery deals in part with aerial spies. This handsome de Havilland DH-4 World War I biplane had two cockpits, enabling the aerial photographer to concentrate on his assignment. The DH-4 was also a favorite plane of an American airmail pilot, Charles Lindbergh.

94 Distinctive German crosses on the wings and tail identify this resplendent Albatros D.Va fighter. World War I ace Manfred von Richthofen, the infamous "Red Baron," achieved most of his 80 scores from an Albatros before he was shot down on April 21, 1918.

95 top Sounds of pounding draw one to the realistic diorama of a 1918 German aircraft factory.

95 bottom Germany's best single-seat fighter in the Great War was the Fokker D.VII. However, it was April 1918 before it engaged in combat. Just two days before the Armistice, this particular Fokker was captured by two quick-thinking Americans, who prevented the enemy pilot from destroying it after he mistakenly landed on an airfield held by the United States.

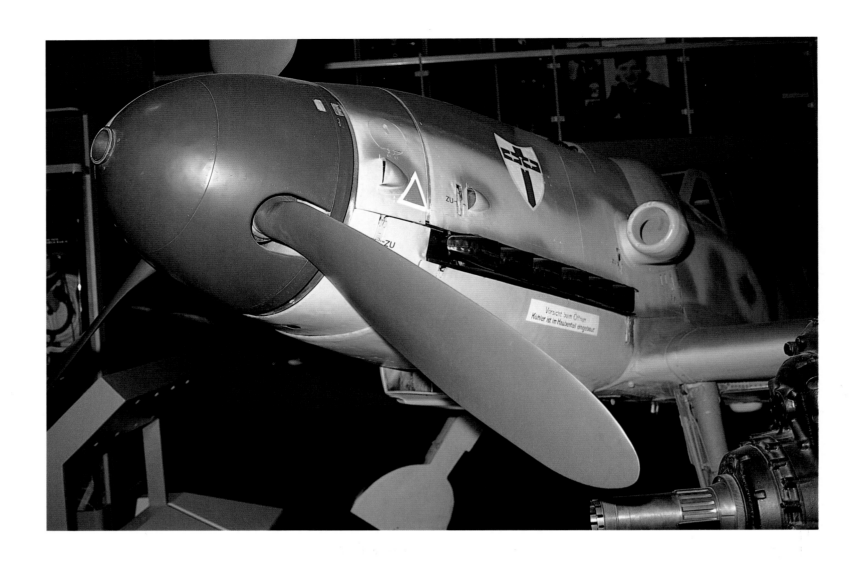

96 Less than 20 years after the German
Fokker D.VII biplane was introduced,
Professor Willy Messerschmitt designed this
trim fighting machine. The most familiar
German plane in World War II, the
Messerschmitt Bf.109G was respected for its
speed, maneuverability and climbing.

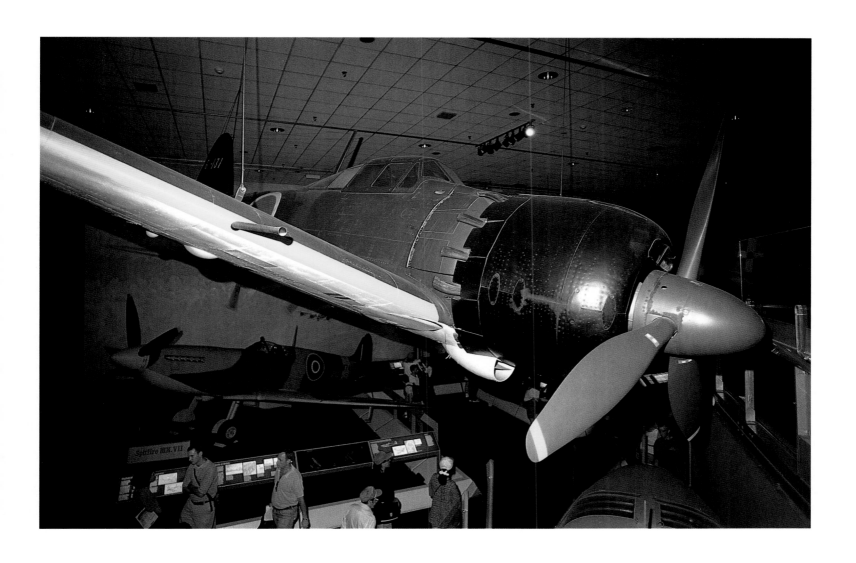

97 The symbol of the rising sun behind and below the cockpit identifies this famous World War II fighter as Japan's Mitsubishi Zero. The A6M5 Model 52 Zero became a formidable foe, capable of heavy firepower, good performance, and agility.

98/99 A gallery devoted to World War II aviation would be incomplete without the B-17 Flying Fortress bomber. Because it was simply too big for the available exhibit space, Keith Ferris painted this striking mural of Boeing B-17s heading home after bombing Wiesbaden, Germany, on August 15, 1944. In the foreground are a British Spitfire at left, and an Italian Macchi suspended over an American Mustang.

100 *This scrappy little British fighter, a*
Supermarine Spitfire Mark VII, served the
Allied cause all over the world. Over 20,000 of
these quick, responsive aircraft had been
manufactured by the end of World War II.
Equipped with eight machine guns, the Spitfire
lived up to its name.

101 Naming and decorating planes with nose art seems to be uniquely American, as illustrated by Willit Run?, North American's P-51D Mustang fighter. Its distinctive black and yellow checkerboard markings denote the 351st Fighter Squadron, 353rd Fighter Group of the Eighth Air Force. Based in England, Mustangs provided escort to bombers crossing the English Channel to Europe.

102/103 Because this Messerschmitt Me 262-1a was the first jet-propelled warplane used in combat, it is displayed in the Jet Aviation gallery. Powered by two turbine engines, its over-500-mph speed outstripped the Mustang by over 100 mph. This version, Schwalbe (Swallow), carried four 30mm cannon. First engaged July 10, 1944, at Javincourt, France, the outcome of the war may have been different had it been in service earlier.

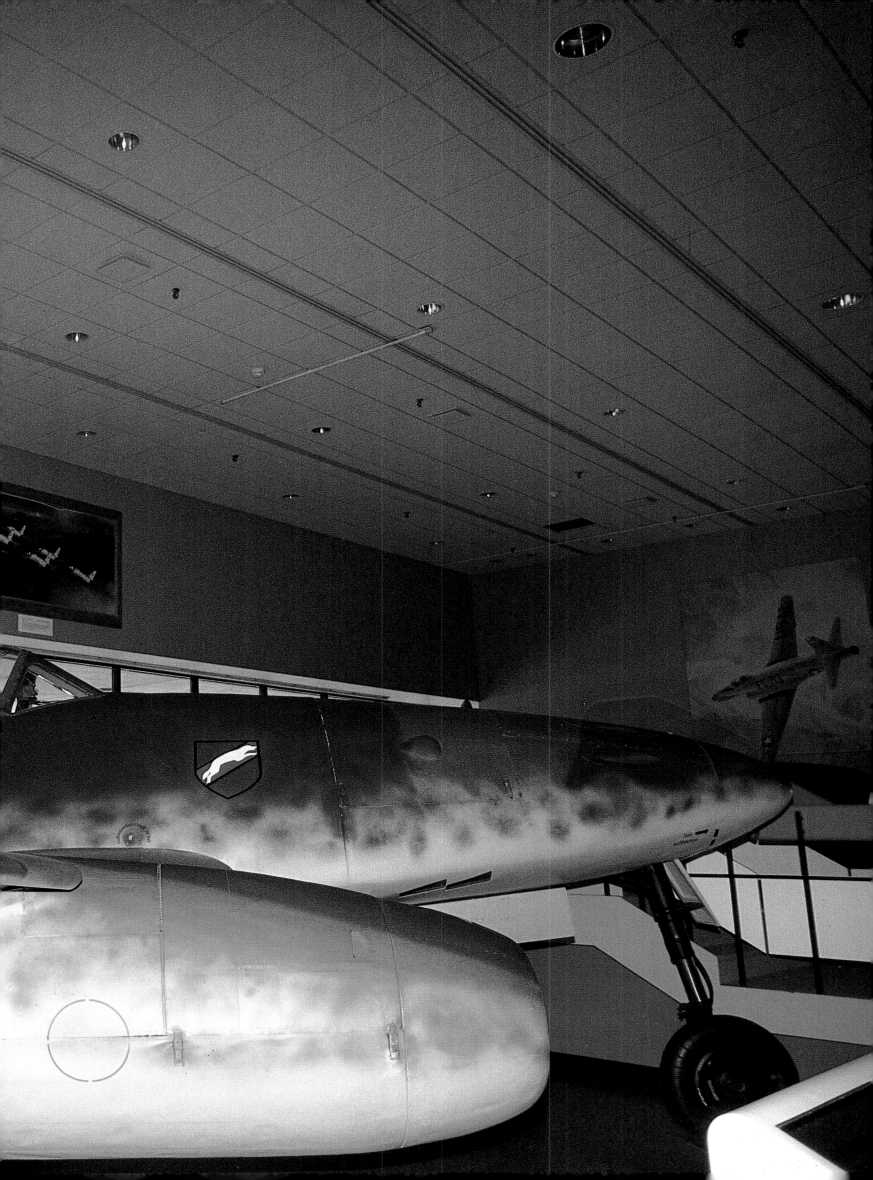

104 With this simulated carrier landing device in Sea-Air Operations, visitors can test their skills landing a plane on an aircraft carrier. A "meatball" or amber light appears on a Fresnel lens. If you are on the glide path, the ball lines up between two horizontal green lines. You needn't be a Top Gun: Nuggets (beginners) and Fleet Pilots (intermediates) can try.

105 In the Jet Aviation gallery, this handsome
McDonnell FH-1 Phantom, with its wings
folded, appears just as it would on a carrier
deck. The first U.S. jet designed for take-offs
and landings on a carrier, the Phantom was
tested aboard the U.S.S. Franklin D.
Roosevelt in July 1946.

106 top Sikorsky is almost synonymous with helicopter. A naturalized American who was born in Kiev, Russia, Igor Ivanovich Sikorsky was one of the foremost developers and designers of helicopters. His XR-4, now in the Vertical Flight gallery, made a record-breaking flight across the United States in 1942.

106 bottom One of many uses for military aircraft is observation. In 1943, this Kellett XO-60 was the seventh and last of the U.S. Army autogiros. The principal difference between autogiros and helicopters is that air flows up through ''windmilling'' autogiro blades and down through powered rotor blades on the helicopter. Helicopters proved superior.

107 This British Hawker XV-6A Kestrel is named for a falcon that can hover in the air with its head to the wind. The vertical and short take-off and landing (V/STOL) Kestrel had rotating engine nozzles that could direct the exhaust downward and create the thrust for a vertical take-off. The Kestrel led directly to the development of the Hawker Siddley Harrier.

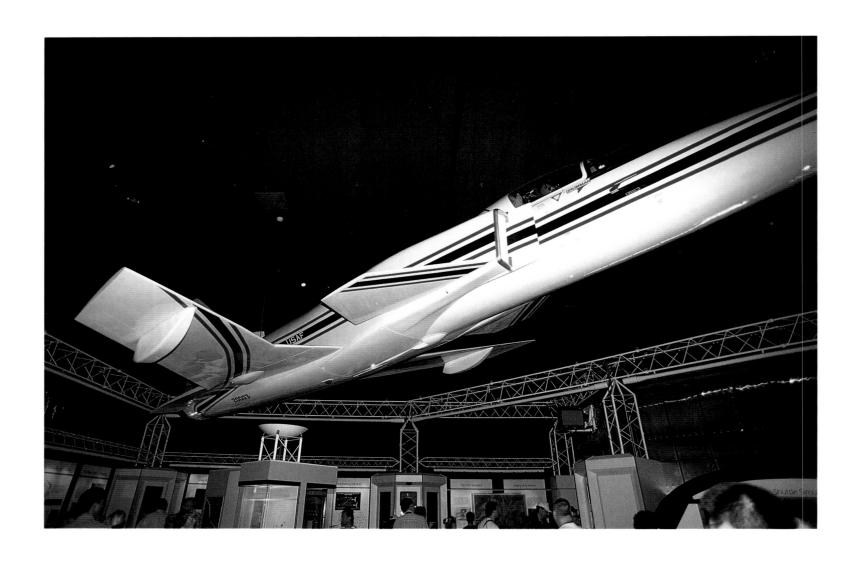

108 As exemplified by an experimental
Grumman X-29, wings that sweep forward –
not back – requiring computer-controlled
stability may be the military aircraft of the
future. First flown in 1984, its radical design is
still being tested. This full-scale steel and
fiberglass mockup was built solely for
exhibition.

109 The exciting Grumman X-29, which
seems to be stabbing through the night sky,
can be studied in the Beyond the Limits
gallery. The subtitle of the gallery announces:
Flight Enters the Computer Age.

QUEST FOR NEW FRONTIERS

The Rocketry and Space Flight gallery begins with a Chinese recipe for gunpowder (potassium nitrate, sulfur and charcoal) from 1040 A.D. and ends with the charred Skylab 4 Apollo Command Module that ferried astronauts to earth after 84 days in space. In a whimsical section, science fiction's Buck Rogers, Flash Gordon and Captain Kirk foreshadow the "science fact" of space travel.

This gallery pulsates with the sounds of rocket engines. Although American Robert Hutchings Goddard is regarded as the father of modern rocketry, two other pioneers conducted independent experiments as well: Russian Konstantin Eduardovitch Tsiolkovsky, who suggested the use of liquid propellants, and Transylvanian Hermann Oberth, whose treatise analyzed technical problems of space flight and proposed a design for spaceships to shelter human beings.

The space age has liberated the ancient science of astronomy from the limitations of earthbound observation. The Stars gallery displays scientific instruments and satellites used to study the sun and stars from space. On exhibit is the fourth component of Skylab, the Apollo Telescope Mount, which photographed the solar corona. "How Big?" uses a clever selection of balls to provide a basis for comparison of stars: a bright yellow Wilson tennis ball makes a good sun, a soccer ball represents Al Na'ir, a basketball, Gamma Apodis.

In the Apollo to the Moon gallery, an ingenious arrangement of mirrors creates the illusion of a cluster of five F-1 rocket engines to reproduce the aft end of the powerful Saturn V rocket, which placed men on the moon. The *Freedom 7* space craft was a tight squeeze for astronaut Alan B. Shepard, on the first successful U.S. suborbital flight on May 7, 1961. In an exhibit on Space Food, the visitor gets an intimate look at the day-to-day provisions, that made up the astronauts' menus. Engagingly sporting a specially designed space suit, the stuffed rhesus monkey, Able, typifies biological experiments prior to man's incursion into space. The feature film, "25 Years of Space Exploration," is a superb review of the events and attitudes of the last quarter-century.

Continuing space probes examine our own galaxy. The Exploring the Planets gallery enables one to put Earth in perspective. An effective use of balls or spheres dramatizes our comparatively diminutive size to that of our neighbors. One could become a philosopher contemplating Jupiter as a thousand Earths. Hovering above is a full-scale replica of Voyagers 1 and 2, hurled on a journey to the outer reaches of our galaxy to transmit back images of Jupiter, Saturn, Uranus and Neptune.

The popular Where Next, Columbus? gallery charts 500 years of exploration and examines the awesome challenges of extended periods in space. It may take three years for a round trip to Mars, but lots of volunteers are willing to risk the physical and psychological stresses. The centerpiece of this area is a walk into Mars, a 3,000-square-foot simulation of rusty-red rocks, alien terrain, robots and adaptive equipment operated by a spaceman.

111 Floating above visitors to the Exploring the Planets gallery, a full-scale engineering test model represents two Voyager spacecraft launched in 1977 to probe the outer planets. Voyager 1 relayed information about Saturn's rings, then left our solar system. Voyager 2 continued to Uranus by January 1986, and in 1989, after 12 years hurtling through space, furnished pictures of Neptune and its moon.

DIRECTING
THE THRUST

TOWARD 2076
THE FUTURE OF
ROCKET PROPULSION

112/113 The Rocketry and Space Flight gallery traces the development of rockets from simple "bottle rockets" to Saturn V, which was capable of sending men to the moon. A display of pressurized and space suits includes the Apollo Portable Life Support System which weighed 104 pounds on Earth and 17 on the moon.

114 The slim Aerobee Nose Cone topped research rockets used in the early 1960s. It contains a group of spectographs in a moving cradle that permitted longer exposure to sunlight for solar observation.

115 One of the stars of the Stars gallery resembles a giant gyroscope. NASA's Orbiting Solar Observatory (OSO) was launched in 1962. As its three arms rotated around the center, OSO examined the Sun in gamma, X-ray and ultraviolet zones of the spectrum.

116/117 The awesome power of a Saturn V rocket is conveyed by this exhibit just beyond the entrance to the Apollo to the Moon gallery. Using one F-1 rocket engine and a unique positioning of mirrors creates the illusion of the five engines required to produce the 7,570,000 pounds of thrust necessary to send men to the moon.

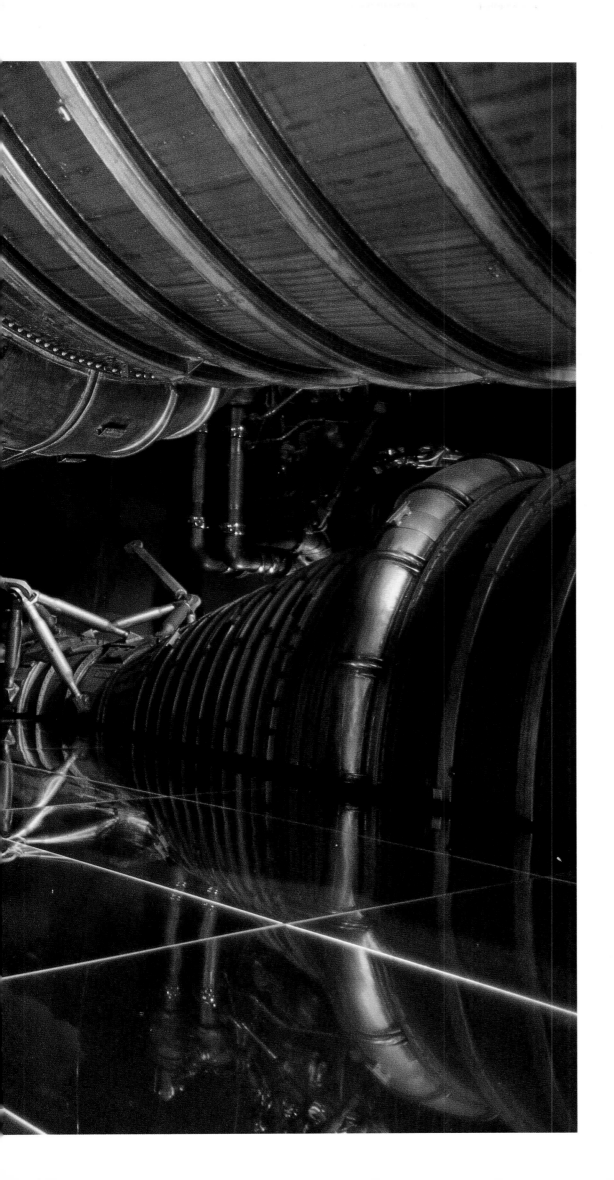

118 On May 5, 1961, less than a month after
Major Yuri Gagarin of Russia orbited the earth,
the U.S. space program, Project Mercury,
launched Freedom 7 on a suborbital flight.
Inside the capsule was Alan Bartlett Shepard,
Jr., America's first man in space.

119 Millions of Americans watched on
television as a Redstone rocket blasted Alan
B. Shepard, Jr. into space from Cape
Canaveral, Florida. This closeup shows the
astronaut tucked inside the capsule. Shepard,
strapped onto a padded fiberglass contoured
couch, could manually control Freedom 7.
The flight lasted 15 minutes and ended 302
miles down range in the Atlantic Ocean.

JUPITER

NEPTUNE

SATURN

URANUS

PLUTO

EARTH

VENUS

SUN

This arc represents a segment of the sun
at the same scale as the models of the
planets. A model of the Sun at this scale
would require a sphere 28 meters (92 feet)
in diameter, and would not fit in this exhibit
gallery.

120 Pointing to the dark blue sphere, a woman indicates to her children the relative position of the Earth to other planets in our solar system. Colored balls graphically illustrate Earth's comparative size to Jupiter, the fifth planet from the sun and largest planet in the solar system.

121 "Buck Rogers in the 25th Century" was exciting stuff in 1929, when Phil Nowlan and Dick Calkins created this popular comic strip. Suddenly youngsters were fascinated by futuristic space travel. A private collection of Buck Rogers toy ray guns, owned by Mrs. Virginia N. Dille, is mounted over an enlargement of the strip.

122 Set against a desolate moonscape, the jeeplike Lunar Roving Vehicle was first used in July 1971, when Apollo 15 astronauts David R. Scott and James B. Irwin covered over 17 miles on the moon. On display is the Lunar Rover similar to one used by Apollo 17, the last manned exploration of the moon, December 1972.

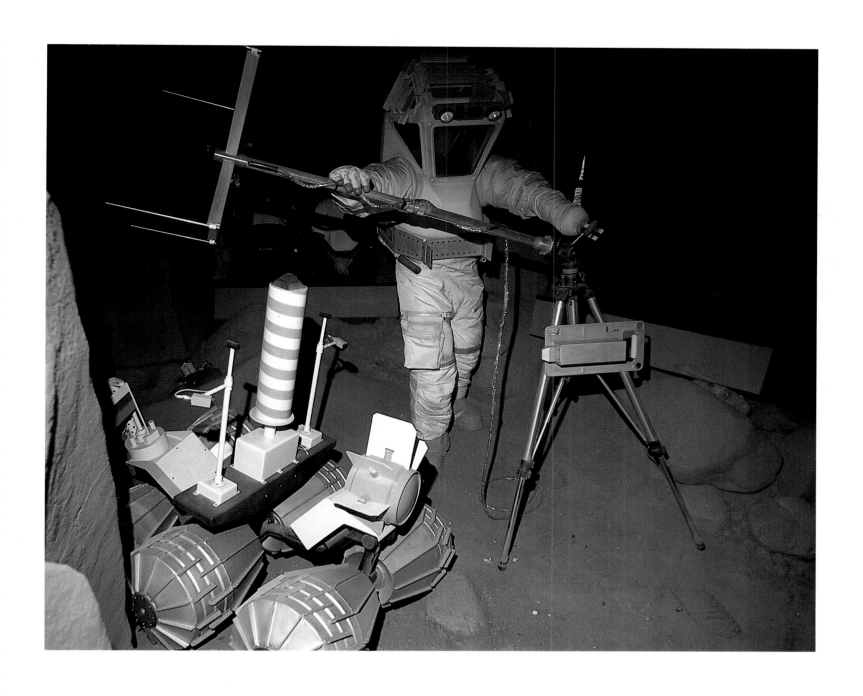

123 Red rocks and desert sand greet a spaceman on Mars. In the Where Next, Columbus? gallery a "Walk into Mars" simulates its hostile environment. The spaceman wears a technologically advanced garment to protect him from extreme night-to-day temperature ranges. At his feet, a full-scale model of a Russian Mars rover, scheduled to be launched in 1996, features specially designed "wheels" to adapt to desert terrain.

In the image: CENTRAL SUPPLIES, UTILITIES ACCESS

124 Here's one way to stay fit in space. Because the body experiences marked physical changes after extended periods of weightlessness – fluids shift; the body replaces less calcium than it removes; there is a reduction in red and white blood cells; and so on – physicians are studying techniques for counteracting these effects.

125 Subjected to intense heat caused by friction with the air as it plunges through the atmosphere, the command module's plastic heat shield melts and slowly vaporizes. Skylab 4's Command Module is blackened and charred, but it safely ferried William R. Pogue, Gerald P. Carr, and Edward G. Gibson to and from their 84-day mission in Skylab's Orbital Workshop.

126/127 The fourth component of Skylab was the Apollo Telescope Mount. Because it contained eight high-resolution telescopes designed for solar observation, this backup is exhibited in the Stars gallery. Each instrument studied a different part of the spectrum: ultraviolet, X-ray, visible, or infrared light.

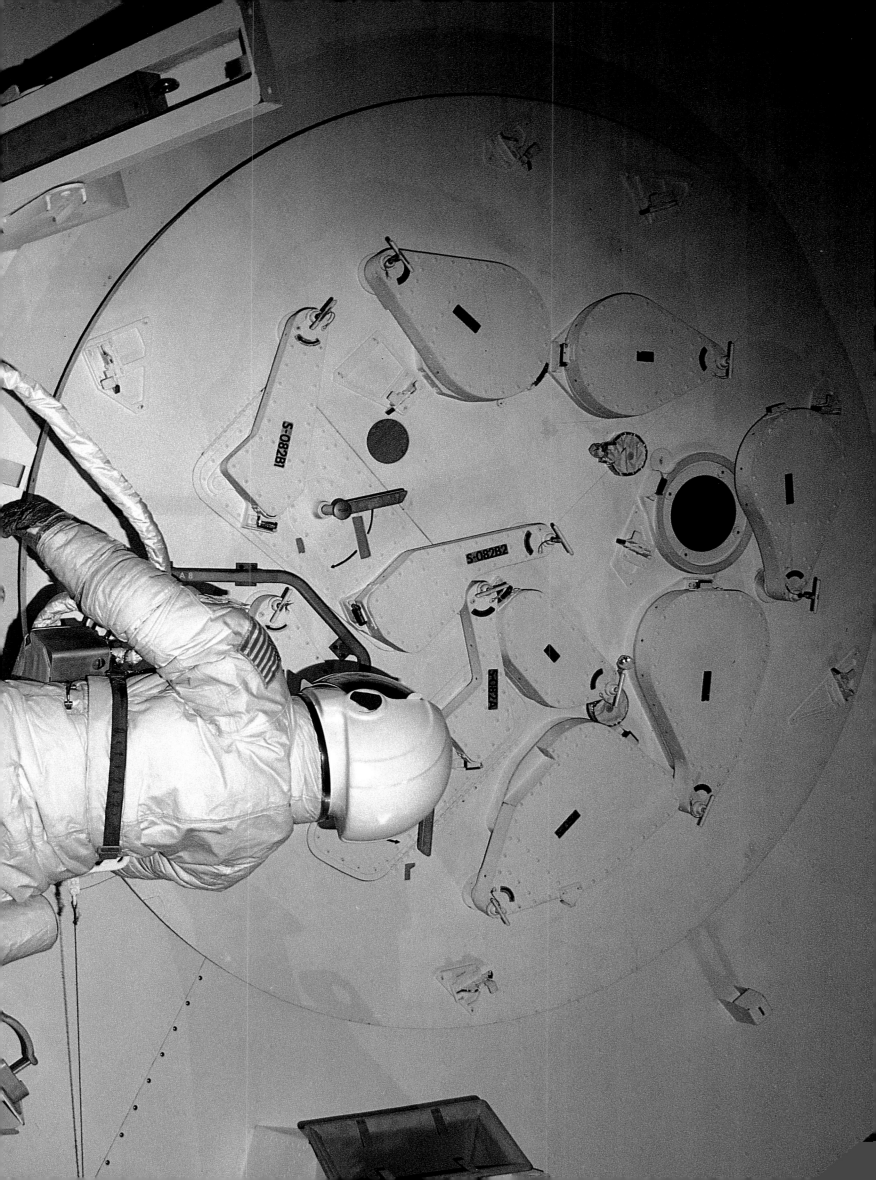